The Wreck of the Oglebay Norton

A history of the rise and demise of Oglebay Norton.

How an ambitious CEO sank a venerable Cleveland company in a sea of red ink

Daniel Warvelle Harbaugh

The Wreck of the Oglebay Norton

Danzmark Productions, Publisher
danzmark@juno.com

LuLu.com , Printer

Special acknowledgement to Mr. Frank Lewis
www.clevescene.com › *News* Sep 22, 2004
for his contribution and the inspiration of this book.

Special thanks to Mr. Ben Young, Noted Author, for
proofing this book.

This book is available on Amazon and at LuLu.com

ISBN 978-1-365-89986-7

9 781365 899867

90000

The Wreck of the Oglebay Norton

TABLE OF CONTENTS

The Wreck of the Oglebay Norton

The Wreck of the Oglebay Norton

FOREWORD

This book is a compilation of articles and data relating to the history of the rise and demise of Oglebay Norton Company of Cleveland , Ohio.

Oglebay Norton was a company engaged in Great Lakes shipping, iron ore and basic metals and mineral-related industries.

"The Wreck of the Oglebay Norton" title is an analogy to the wreck of O-N flagship **SS Edmund Fitzgerald** that sank in a violent storm in **November 10, 1975**, and was memorialized in the ballad by Gordon Lightfoot   "The Wreck of the Edmund Fitzgerald".

Like the Titanic sailing on to disaster heedless of icebergs, Oglebay Norton sailed on heedless of economic icebergs.

John Lauer was 59 when he took the helm at Oglebay Norton in 1998, and 64 at his departure in 2003. Presumably he went down with the ship careerwise.

The old adage ..."There are two sides to every story" .. is undoubtedly applicable. The fact that John. Lauer 'put his money where his mouth is' indicates he had the best of intentions. Perhaps someday he will tell his side.

Daniel Warvelle Harbaugh

The Wreck of the Oglebay Norton

The Wreck of the Oglebay Norton

TIMETABLE:

Five years on the voyage to disaster under Captain John N. Lauer.

January 1, 1998: The Board of Directors of Oglebay Norton Company named John N. Lauer as President and Chief Executive Officer and a member of the Board.

From continuing operations of $239 million in 1998. Under Mr. Lauer's leadership, Oglebay Norton doubled its size in 1998 with the acquisitions of:

Global Stone Corporation

Port Inland Limestone Company

Colorado Silica Sand

Franklin Industries' Mica Business

iller Products Company

Including these acquisitions, Oglebay Norton's pro forma revenues for 1998 totaled $288 million.

Shareholders, watched the stock price dwindle from a high of $50 to mere pennies.

Oglebay Norton entered into Chapter 11 bankruptcy on Feb. 23, 2004.

The Wreck of the Oglebay Norton

A reorganization plan was approved by a bankruptcy court on Nov. 17, 2004, and the company legally emerged from Chapter 11 on Jan. 31, 2005.

2008: Oglebay Norton was acquired by Carmeuse Lime & Stone, Inc. .

Carmeuse Lime

Caramus Lime acquired Oglebay Norton in 2008 . Caramuse had a 150 year history coincident with Oglebay Norton's.   Caramuse successfully navigated the business seas that sank Ogilby Norton. Oglebay Norton CEO John Lauer presumable has reflected on what Caramuse dod right and what he did wrong.

Carmeuse Lime & Stone is the North American subsidiary of Belgium-based Carmeuse . It supplies lime and limestone products in North America, producing some 7 million tons annually of lime products and around 25 million tons of limestone aggregates and chemical limestone from roughly 30 plants. It makes quicklime (calcium oxide), dolomitic lime (a mixture of calcium carbonate and magnesium carbonate), milk of lime, and hydrated lime (calcium hydroxide). Industrial customers use Carmeuse Lime & Stone's mineral products in steel production, water treatment, road construction, heavy construction, and other applications. The company primarily sells its products in the eastern US and Canada.

The Wreck of the Oglebay Norton

How an ambitious CEO sank a venerable Cleveland company in a sea of red ink.

By Frank Lewis
www.clevescene.com › *News* Sep 22, 2004

In nearly a century and a half in Great Lakes shipping and mining, Oglebay Norton Co. never had a CEO quite like John Lauer.

When the former B.F. Goodrich leader joined Oglebay in late 1997, he refused to accept a salary. At the time, Lauer was a doctoral candidate at Case Western Reserve University, and his thesis was on one of the hot-button issues of the day: executive pay -- and the excesses thereof. So in a commendable display of practicing what one preaches, Lauer opted for performance-based bonuses and stocks in lieu of a paycheck. He also purchased $1 million in company stock. Lauer was taking a multi-million-dollar gamble on himself.

When we put the deal together," Lauer told the Associated Press in 1998, "the way we designed it was that I wouldn't get credit for market momentum. I'd get credit for true growth."

The Wreck of the Oglebay Norton

And growth is what Oglebay got. Traditionally focused on ore mining and shipping, Oglebay would leave ore and the fading steel industry behind in favor of lime, limestone, and sand. *Surveyor*, a publication of the American Bureau of Shipping, summed up the transition in 2001: "What began as an ore company that also had boats, and became a steamship company that also had minerals, is now a stone company that also has boats."

Revenues soared, and Oglebay rose steadily up the Weatherhead 100, Case's annual ranking of Northeast Ohio's fastest-growing businesses, going from 20th in 1999 to 4th in 2002. The value of Oglebay shares -- long an unexciting but reliable "widows and orphans stock," as one longtime holder puts it -- reached previously unimaginable heights. Lauer's vision of building the sleepy, narrowly focused company into a billion-dollar behemoth actually seemed plausible. And through it all, his reputation soared.

He was featured in numerous national publications and hailed as a new breed of leader in a best-selling management book. The AFL-CIO declared him a "CEO pay hero."

The Wreck of the Oglebay Norton

But his plan was built on the New Economy, which meant rapid expansion and equally frantic borrowing – in this case, hundreds of millions of dollars. Yet as the New Economy began to look hopelessly naive, so did Lauer's plans for Oglebay. It was one thing to assume the stock market would rise forever, as many business leaders did. It was quite another to believe, as Lauer apparently did, that the company would integrate its new operations quickly, and that rapid growth would allow rapid repayment of debt. He was wrong. The debt began to weigh down the company like flooding in a ship's hull. Last February, Oglebay Norton – once "the most conservative, risk-averse company that ever existed," according to one analyst – filed for bankruptcy.

Oglebay management predicts that a stronger company will emerge. But it's in their interests to focus on the future.

Shareholders, who have watched the stock price dwindle from a high of $50 to mere pennies,

 still have questions about the past. Most pertain to Lauer, and what, if anything, the board of directors did to make sure investors' interests were protected.

The Wreck of the Oglebay Norton

Of course, many of these same shareholders weren't so curious about the inner workings when their stock was ascending. But they note that the company, founded in the mid-19th century,

had already survived depression, countless market swings, wars, and technological revolutions. In just a few heady years under Lauer, it collapsed. Even in the Rust Belt, its disintegration stands out.

"They took a magnificent company, one of the bedrock companies of Northeast Ohio's economy, and they ruined it," says shareholder Douglas Barr.

The company that would become Oglebay Norton was established in 1851 and quickly moved into the growing iron-ore market.

In 1855, it employed then-unknown John D. Rockefeller as a bookkeeper at $3.50 a week. "The three and a half years of business training I had in that commission house formed a large part of the foundation of my business career," he wrote years later. In the 1890s, Oglebay, Norton and Company acted as the sales and shipping agent for Rockefeller's Lake Superior Consolidated Iron Mines.

Rockefeller sold his mines and ships to United States Steel in 1901, but Oglebay carried on,

The Wreck of the Oglebay Norton

managing mines and buying and building ships to haul raw materials over the Great Lakes. Decades of high demand for steel -- fueled by the rise of the automobile and two world wars - kept the company busy, as did forays into coal and taconite. In 1957, it absorbed some of its affiliates, adopted the name Oglebay Norton Company, and began trading publicly.

Oglebay's last brush with unwanted attention came with the sinking of the *Edmund Fitzgerald* amid freakishly bad weather on Lake Superior in 1975.

Oglebay operated the ship for owner Northwestern Mutual Life Insurance Company. All 29 crew members died.

In the early 1990s, Oglebay began moving away from industries like coal and iron ore. Today, the company mines and processes lime and limestone for the construction, environmental, and metallurgical industries, in addition to sands and specialty minerals used in everything from paint to oil-drilling operations. The company also owns and operates a 12-ship Great Lakes fleet, which in 1996 hauled 22 million tons.

Come the late '90s, however, the board had grown restless, according to several sources. Exactly how and when John Lauer came into the picture isn't clear; neither he nor any current board members responded to interview requests. But by late 1997, R. Thomas Green, who'd been president and CEO since 1992, was out, and Lauer was in.

"He had an excellent reputation," says Harry Millis, a retired analyst who followed both Oglebay and the tire industry, in which Lauer had previously worked as president of B.F. Goodrich.

There was some speculation that Lauer left Goodrich because he wasn't aggressive enough for the company's board, Millis says. Lauer's own accounts don't shed much light. A 1998 *Fortune* profile said he left "in hope of becoming a CEO elsewhere or launching his own company." But a 2002 *Harvard Business Review* article said the "inspirational leader" had "lost his spark" after six years of meetings and memos: "Over time, Lauer had fallen in step with a corporate culture that was focused on shareholder value in a way that was inconsistent with what he cared about. Not surprisingly, he left the company six months later, breaking from corporate life by joining his wife with her work with Hungarian relief organizations."

The Wreck of the Oglebay Norton

An extended timeout ensued, during which he "wanted nothing to do with running a company," the article said. Instead he pursued an executive doctorate at Case. He was wrapping up his dissertation -- on how multimillion-dollar CEO salaries hurt employee morale and productivity -- when Oglebay came calling.

The board loved his revolutionary notion of being paid only for performance.

"It generates instant respect," said director James Bartlett in a 1998 *Fortune* article. "The word was out that we had a leader who was willing to put himself on the line, and that this will be a damn interesting place to work."

And it was. Armed with a mandate for change, Lauer set to work realizing his vision of dramatic expansion -- the kind that would attract attention from big-time investors. Oglebay bought small competitor Colorado Silica, an industrial sands company. Then it entered the lime and limestone market by acquiring three companies, including Global Stone Corporation, the fifth-largest lime and limestone producer in North America, for $226 million. The combination of these acquisitions immediately constituted Oglebay's largest division.

The Wreck of the Oglebay Norton

But by June '98, the company's debt had risen from $45 million the previous year to more than $300 million. At the annual shareholders' meeting the following month, Lauer laid out his plan for further expansion and the achievement of $1 billion in revenues -- up from $145 million in '97 -- by 2000. He was elected chairman of the board.

A year later Oglebay bought another company's mineral assets and created Oglebay Norton Specialty Mineral. The spending binge continued throughout 2000. Michigan Limestone Operations in April. Jebco Abrasives of Texas in June. A property of J.M. Huber Limestone of Indiana in September. All for cash.

"He'd buy almost anything," recalls Brent Baird, a former board member from Buffalo, still sounding incredulous years later. "And it was all with borrowed money."

Baird, who'd joined the board around 1990 after buying more than 500,000 shares, says he supported "the first one or two" acquisitions, but started asking questions as the frenzy continued -- and the debt mounted. "When I was first with the company, we didn't have a lot of debt,"

he explains. "I'm a conservative guy; I don't like to pay money to banks."

The first time Baird raised these concerns, Lauer talked about growth and diversification, and most board members -- "the Cleveland old boys' network," as Baird puts it -- seemed content. The next time Baird asked questions, Lauer got "nasty." A heated exchange ensued.

"Lauer would do that if you challenged him," says John Weil, a former board member and shareholder from St. Louis, who also grew skeptical over time. He recalls Lauer's response to Baird: "Why'd you hire me if you wanted me to be a custodial manager?"

Driving home after that meeting, Baird thought, "This is nuts. I'm gonna quit." Once the second-largest stockholder, he opted not to stand for reelection to the board and began selling his shares as soon as the law allowed. Weil, who owned about 600,000 shares, became the sole vocal dissenter on the board.

At a meeting in St. Louis shortly after the Michigan Limestone deal, Weil says, Lauer talked about pushing earnings to heights unheard of at the long-sleepy company.

Only later did Weil learn that Lauer's earnings projections hadn't taken into account routine off-season maintenance at Michigan Limestone or that the economy was showing signs of softening. "I began worrying that the board wasn't getting the full story," he says.

Others wonder whether most board members even wanted the full story.

Lauer's moves made sense at the time, says Millis, the analyst who followed Oglebay. "I don't think anyone questioned the strategy or the individual acquisitions at the time they were done," he says. Indeed, Wall Street "applauded," with rising stock prices. In June 2000, BB&T Capital Markets strongly advised its clients to buy Oglebay stock, calling it "compellingly" undervalued.

"Oglebay has achieved strong competitive positions with these acquisitions . . . The transition at Oglebay is likely the cause of some skepticism and uncertainty among investors . . . [The] transition has put the company in two seemingly distinct lines of business, shipping and minerals . . . The increased degree of leverage does raise Oglebay's risk profile .

If the company achieves goals, then it will have compounded earnings at an annual rate of 15 percent."

The Wreck of the Oglebay Norton

In other words, the company was poised for tremendous growth . . . or an ugly fall. And that's when forces began to turn against it.

In 2000 and 2001, the water levels in the Great Lakes dropped to their lowest in decades, limiting the amount of tonnage Oglebay's ships could carry without running aground. At the same time, fuel costs rose, further eating into profits. Lauer remained optimistic, however, predicting revenue of $425 million to $440 million for 2001, up from 2000's $393 million.

Lauer's strategy was to acquire companies within or closely related to Oglebay's expertise and run them more efficiently as a group than they could operate freestanding. "Like Ford buying GM and Chrysler," says Scott Thompson, a director at financial crisis-management adviser Alvarez and Marsal in New York. A Ford-GM-Chrysler megacorporation merger would have one headquarters, not three; one human-resources department, not three, and so forth.

The key is to take advantage of all the cost savings. (Thompson held Oglebay stocks left to him by his grandfather, who was the company's lawyer for many years.)

The Wreck of the Oglebay Norton

But there were flaws in the plan. First, Oglebay paid peak prices, because the economy was strong and mergers and acquisitions were occurring everywhere; many companies were overvalued in the late '90s, Thompson notes.

Still, the seemingly boundless economic growth at the time made the risk appear manageable. "You see that a lot with these smaller companies," says Dominick D'Ascoli, an analyst with Standard & Poor who followed Oglebay. "They miscalculate the market going forward." And when the economy goes south, the debt becomes more of a burden than they're prepared to carry.

The first half of 2001 was rough. In July, Oglebay was forced to admit that earnings for the year would be well below those of 2000. In September, it warned that business would not improve until the economy recovered. And in October, Oglebay stopped paying dividends to shareholders, sending the stock price into free fall.

The following month, Lauer lost one of his titles. Michael Lundin, who'd come to Oglebay in the Michigan Limestone deal, was named president. It was the start of a tumultuous year and a half.

The Wreck of the Oglebay Norton

Early in 2002, Oglebay acquired yet another company -- Erie Sand & Gravel. A few months later, Oglebay announced that Lundin would succeed Lauer as CEO at the end of the year. Lauer would remain chairman of the board. Before that happened, however, the company secured $75 million in financing at a whopping 18 percent interest. Awash in debt, management was playing for time.

By the April 2003 annual meeting, shareholders were restless. Days before, Thompson shared with Douglas Barr, a shareholder with old family ties to the company, the results of an informal analysis he'd done: "As I calculate . . . all cash flow from operations over the next two years (at a very minimum) will go to pay interest and cover necessary capital expenditures, with nothing left over to reduce debt," he wrote. By 2004, he predicted, the company could have paid well over $60 million in interest.

He offered suggestions drawn from his experience with struggling companies, but noted: "I don't expect my ideas to be popular with management or the board, as [they] would require an attitude change from grandeur to restructuring and could be viewed as an admission of failure."

At the meeting, Lundin was asked if he'd consulted bankruptcy attorneys. He said no. But Lundin later admitted that he had spoken to lawyers about a bankruptcy filing, says Barr.

The real intrigue involved Lauer. Two hours after being reelected chairman of the board, he resigned. Board member Al Bersticker, who'd met privately with Lauer before the surprise announcement (and who became the next chairman), would not explain what happened. "We thank John for his service, dedication, and leadership at Oglebay Norton," he said in a statement, "and we wish him well in his future endeavors."

In May 2003, Geoffrey Seymour, a trustee for nearly 150,000 shares of Oglebay stock, wrote to Bersticker, seeking explanation for "the substantial and unacceptable loss of value of this holding." He itemized a list of questions, but the first one got right to the heart of the matter: "Specifically, how did you act to safeguard shareholder value in approving this debt increase?"

The Wreck of the Oglebay Norton

Seymour says that Bersticker called to say he was aware of the board's responsibilities. But wouldn't say how it had filled them, nor did he address any other concerns.

Seymour's experience wasn't unique.

As the company's distress became obvious, the board increasingly hid from shareholders and the media. There was no annual meeting this year. And when Douglas Barr, whose wife is a descendant of earlier Oglebay executives, sent identical letters to all board members last October, asking many pointed questions, the only response came from Lundin. "[T]he board has created a formal policy stating that the president and CEO is responsible for all public disclosure and communication," he wrote. But Lundin didn't answer most of Barr's questions, claiming that Barr was "not seeking factual information, but rather opinion and in some instances speculative analysis."

The board's silence only encouraged shareholders to blame them for Oglebay's state.

"As near as I can tell, they did nothing to rein [Lauer] in," Barr says. To him and many other shareholders, the board's stewardship was, at best, unconscionably shortsighted. That board

The Wreck of the Oglebay Norton

members have refused to buy stock in the company in recent years, despite being urged to by Barr and others, compounds their frustration. (Barr says that one member bluntly stated that it was a bad investment. Another begged off by claiming a shortage of cash: "Doug, I'm building a very expensive house in Phoenix.")

"I've got a general picture, which is pretty abominable," says Robert Crawford of St. Louis, who's owned a few thousand shares for two decades. In 50 years of investing, he says, "I've never seen anything like this before."

"It was a good, solid company, and it was like a family almost," says Thomas Thompson, a Columbus attorney. "It's sad to see a business with that much tradition die as it did."

The business has not died, but for longtime shareholders, it might as well have. From decades of no-frills stability to the once-unimaginable stock price of $50 per share to the equally incomprehensible bankruptcy

and a NASDAQ delisting just a few short years later, it's been like watching the quick demise of a beloved relative.

The Wreck of the Oglebay Norton

Shareholders have formed an informal network and support group, scrutinizing new developments and piecing together unconfirmed bits and pieces. One rumor bouncing between them in the spring turned out to be true: There have been offers to buy Oglebay's assets. In March, a group led by Lafarge North America, the continent's largest supplier of construction materials, informed Oglebay's bankruptcy lawyer of its interest. Nathan Creech, Lafarge's director of business development, declined comment.

Two of those prospective buyers resurfaced later in another consortium. In July, Cleveland attorney Thomas Coffey confirmed that a group including two names well-known at Oglebay -- R. Thomas Green, who was replaced by Lauer, and Renold Thompson Jr., son of the CEO who preceded Green -- made an offer of $451 million. This consortium would break up the company, but operations currently based in Cleveland would stay. (Renold Thompson -- no relation to Thomas and Scott -- did not respond to interview requests. Green "regretfully" declined to comment, citing ongoing talks.)

To shareholders, $451 million sounds like a good deal -- certainly better than what Oglebay's plan offers them: first crack at a limited number of new shares when the company emerges from bankruptcy. Oglebay Vice President and General Counsel Rochelle Walk calls this a "gift": Typically, in bankruptcies like this one, shareholders get nothing.

This too they might see as a gift, though one of little value: The board of directors will be replaced.

To Michael Lundin, Lauer's hand-picked successor, falls the unenviable task of righting the ship.

No one wanted to file for bankruptcy, says Michael Lundin in an interview in his North Point Tower office. But by late 2003, it was becoming increasingly clear that a Chapter 11 reorganization was "the most viable option to sustain the company going forward."

After Oglebay was forced to seek new terms for debt repayment, its bankers demanded a $100 million reduction in debt by February 2004. The company hired a financial adviser to explore selling some assets, such as the mica and lime operations, but the offers were insufficient. (The mica asset remains on the market.)

 Oglebay eventually sold a lawn-and-garden-products business, but this barely put a dent in the debt.

The Wreck of the Oglebay Norton

"We reached out to the marketplace to get their input," says Lundin, referring to the shopping of some assets. "And it was only after that process that we concluded that we needed to file for [bankruptcy] protection."

But that process, he adds, has offered a validation of sorts. The company entered bankruptcy with a new $75 million credit package, then secured another $305 million to pay off its former bank group and reemerge from Chapter 11. "We have good core businesses," Lundin says, "and the market has recognized that and is validating that."

Despite formal objections from some shareholders and the Green-Thompson consortium -- both parties complained that Oglebay was disclosing far less about its assets and liabilities than bankruptcy law requires -- the company's plan was largely approved by a bankruptcy judge in July. Lundin says the company has met with the consortium of prospective buyers and takes the offer seriously, but "We have a plan, and we are committed to that plan." Last week, company spokesman Patrick Gallagher confirmed that talks with the consortium were ongoing, but that a deal remained unlikely. A final hearing on Oglebay's reorganization plan is scheduled for September 29.

The Wreck of the Oglebay Norton

And after that? "We're going to be more focused" on the core businesses, specifically limestone. He is careful not to sound disparaging of decisions made on Lauer's watch, but admits the current plan is "clearly a different strategy."

I'm an engineer, and engineers tend to look at things in a very quantitative way, but the world doesn't really operate like that," John Lauer said in a 2002 interview with *Human Resource Executive* magazine. "There's a lot of change and ambiguity."

The article goes on to describe Lauer's experiences with "emotional intelligence," a psychologically influenced take on management that emphasizes careful self-assessment, better listening skills, and delegation. Richard Boyatzis, a Case professor and co-author of the book *Primal Leadership: Realizing the Power of Emotional Intelligence*, helped Lauer organize Oglebay's management through "a series of customized courses that included case studies from the company, courses in EI taught by Boyatzis,

and in-depth self-assessments by each manager -- with the assistance of a coach -- of their own leadership styles and goals," the story noted.

The Wreck of the Oglebay Norton

Yet it failed to mention that, by the time it was published, Lauer had already stepped down as president, and Oglebay was hurtling toward bankruptcy.

Today, shareholders can take some satisfaction from knowing that Lauer will lose his $9,000-per-month retirement payment as part of the company's reorganization. He would have had to live a long time to make the millions he could have demanded in traditional salary and bonuses, anyway. But perhaps that's a small price to pay for taking a venerable company down with him.
"He looked like a great guy," says former board member Weil. "He just seemed not to understand leverage."

The Wreck of the Oglebay Norton

John N. Lauer

Born: c. 1939

Gender: Male
Race or Ethnicity: White
Occupation: Business

Nationality: United States
Executive summary: CEO of Oglebay Norton, 1997-2002

University: BS Chemical Engineering, University of Maryland College Park (1963)
University: MBA, Texas A&M University Kingsville

Oglebay Norton Co. CEO (1997-2002)
Goodrich President and COO (1990-94)
Goodrich EVP (1989-90)
Celanese VP Engineering Plastics Group
Member of the Board of Diebold (1992-, as Chairman, 2005-)
Member of the Board of Oglebay Norton Co. (as Chairman, 1997-2003)
Opera Cleveland Trustee
Sigma Alpha Epsilon Fraternity
University of Maryland Foundation Board of Directors

John N. Lauer's Biography

2005 - Present: Non-executive Chairman of the Board, Diebold, Incorporated; May 2003: Retired Chairman of the Board, Oglebay Norton Co., Cleveland, Ohio (industrial minerals). Member of our Board Governance and Compensation Committees. Mr. Lauer's experience as a former Chief Executive Officer of a global manufacturing company, with extensive experience in Europe and Asia Pacific, brings directly relatable experience to our Board. Further, during his 18 years on our Board, Mr. Lauer has provided demonstrated leadership to our Board. Mr. Lauer's background as a board chairman of two global corporations also provides significant corporate ...

Source: Diebold on 03/14/2012

Lauer In ...

Oglebay Norton Company Names John Lauer as President, CEO; Succeeds Thomas Green, Who Will Retire. Board and new CEO structure innovative stock-only compensation package.

Dec 17, 1997, from Oglebay Norton Company

CLEVELAND, Dec. 17 /PRNewswire/ – The Board of Directors of Oglebay Norton Company (Nasdaq: OGLE) today named John N. Lauer as President and Chief Executive Officer and a member of the Board, effective January 1, 1998.

Lauer, former President and Chief Operating officer of The B.F.Goodrich Company, will also become a significant shareholder of Oglebay Norton and will be named Chairman at the Company's April 29 annual meeting. Lauer succeeds Chairman R. Thomas Green Jr., a 32-year veteran of the Company who plans to retire in April. Green, who has been Chairman, President and CEO since 1992, will continue to serve as a director of the Board.

Oglebay Norton provides Great Lakes marine transportation, the mining and marketing of industrial sands, and the manufacturing and marketing of engineered materials for the steel, oil and gas, ceramic, chemical, glass, electric utility and construction industries. The Company had revenues of $160.7 million in 1996.

"I am excited to be joining Oglebay Norton as it stands primed for a period of accelerated growth," said Lauer. "

"Over the past several years, Tom Green has done an outstanding job of establishing a strong operational platform on which to build. His success is reflected in this year's higher levels of tonnage hauled and products shipped, improved margins, increased profits, enhanced share price and decreased debt."

Green said, "I am proud of what our people have accomplished in making Oglebay Norton a leaner, more efficient and competitive company than ever before by repositioning of the Company. As a result, by year-end 1997 we will have produced five straight years of improved earnings and increase shareholder wealth."

In making the announcement, the Board noted that Lauer brings both the operational and experience that will help take Oglebay Norton to the "next level. He is well-respected for his vision and his ability to successfully integrate related businesses to maximize the synergies and efficiencies.

The Wreck of the Oglebay Norton

While Lauer said he envisions Oglebay Norton as a $1 billion company "early in the new millennium both through acquisitions and internal growth, he said specific goals and objectives will take shape during his first 90 days as CEO.

"My objective will be to create an aggressive but doable growth strategy with a well understood and monitored execution timetable," he said. "With increased focus companywide, we will place greater emphasis on growth and shareholder value enhancement, while continuing excellent customer service and employee well-being."

Lauer said he will invest $1 million of his own funds in Oglebay Norton

shares. The Company will match his investment with restricted shares. Lauer will not receive any cash compensation. In addition to the Company's match of his investment, if certain aggressive performance criteria are met, Lauer will be able to exercise performance shares providing him with an outright ownership in the Company of an additional 8 percent at the end of five years.

Oglebay Norton has approximately 4.7 million shares outstanding.

The Wreck of the Oglebay Norton

Since retiring from BFGoodrich in 1995, Lauer, 58, has pursued personal investment interests and has worked closely with Primus Venture Partners of Cleveland and Bessemer Holdings, LP of New York in an attempt to acquire a chemical enterprise. He currently serves on the boards of Diebold Incorporated, Canton, Ohio; Menasha Corporation, Neenah, Wisconsin; and BorsodChem Rt, Kazincbarcika, Hungary. He also chairs the Board of Visitors at the University of Maryland and is chair of the Visiting Nurse Association of Cleveland Hospice.

Lauer joined BFGoodrich in 1989 as Executive Vice President in charge of corporate environmental health and safety and as president of what was thenits $1 billion Geon Vinyl Division. He was elected to the Board of Directors later that year.

In 1990, he was promoted to President and Chief Operating Officer, with responsibility for the $1.1 billion Aerospace and $1.25 billion Specialty Chemicals businesses as well as environmental health and safety, corporate research and development, and technology equity investments.

Earlier in his career, Lauer headed marketing and sales for Celanese Chemical Co., served as President of Celanese Specialty Operations and was President of Hoechst Celanese Engineering Resins & Hoechst,

AG, where he was responsible for the consolidation and integration of Hoechst AG's worldwide Engineering Thermoplastics Business.

Lauer, who is currently completing an executive doctorate in management at Case Western Reserve University's Weatherhead School of Management, holds a master's in Business Administration degree from Texas A&M University at Kingsville and a bachelor's degree in Chemical Engineering from the University of Maryland at College Park. He and his wife, Edith, founder and president ofthe Hungarian-American Coalition, reside in Shaker Heights, Ohio.

Green, 60, joined Oglebay Norton in 1965 as a sales representative in the Iron Ore Department. After a series of other management positions, including a period in Zanesville, Ohio, as President of the Central Silica Co. subsidiary, he returned to Cleveland and became Vice President-Iron Ore Operations, which included management responsibility for the $200 million Eveleth Mine operations in Minnesota. He was elected Executive Vice President

in 1990 and promoted to Chairman, President and CEO in 1992.

Green is a member of the Board of Directors of The Steel Alliance and atrustee of the Lake Carriers Association. He also serves on the Executive

Committee of the Greater Cleveland Growth Association, the Executive Committee of the Amherst College Alumni Association,

and on the boards of Hiram College and Western Reserve Academy as well as the Diocesan Council of the Episcopal Diocese of Ohio.

Lauer out at Oglebay

May 01, 2003 Updated 4/30/2003

Just five months after relinquishing the job of CEO, John Lauer has resigned as chairman of Oglebay Norton Co. (Nasdaq: OGLE)
Oglebay Norton said Mr. Lauer also resigned as a director of the supplier of industrial minerals and aggregates. Oglebay Norton said the board elected Albert Bersticker as its non-executive chairman. Mr. Bersticker is a retired chairman and CEO of Ferro Corp. He has served on the Oglebay Norton board since 1992 and has been lead director of the board since 1999.

No reason was given for Mr. Lauer's sudden resignation as chairman. Mr. Bersticker said, "We thank John for his service, dedication and leadership at Oglebay Norton, and we wish him well in his future endeavors."

The Wreck of the Oglebay Norton

Mr. Lauer retired as Oglebay Norton's president in November 2001 and as CEO in December 2002. He was succeeded in both positions by the current president and CEO, Michael Lundin.

Oglebay Norton earlier this week posted a $10 million loss for the first quarter, and recently had to ask its bank lenders to waive certain covenants in its lending agreement.

After the relatively mild 1990 recession ended in early 1992, the country hit a belated unemployment rate peak of 7.8% in mid-1992. Job growth was initially muted by large layoffs among defense related industries.[1] However, payrolls accelerated in 1992 and experienced robust growth through the year 2000.[2]

Predictions that the bubble would burst emerged during the dot-com bubble in the late 1990s. Predictions about a future burst increased following the October 27, 1997 mini-crash, in the wake of the Asian crisis. This caused an uncertain economic climate during the first few months of 1998. However conditions improved, and the Federal Reserve raised interest rates six times between June 1999 and May 2000 in an effort to cool the economy to achieve a soft landing.

The Wreck of the Oglebay Norton

The burst of the stock market bubble occurred in the form of the NASDAQ crash in March 2000. Growth in gross domestic product slowed considerably in the third quarter of 2000 to the lowest rate since a contraction in the first quarter of 1992.

The NBER's Business Cycle Dating Committee has determined that a peak in business activity occurred in the U.S. economy in March 2001. A peak marks the end of an expansion and the beginning of a recession. The determination of a peak date in March is thus a determination that the expansion that began in March 1992ended in March 2001 and a recession began [1]. The expansion lasted almost 10 years, the longest in the NBER's chronology [2]. According to the National Bureau of Economic Research (NBER), which is the private, nonprofit, nonpartisan organization charged with determining economic recessions, the U.S. economy was in recession from March 2001 to November 2001 [3], a period of eight months at the beginning of President George W. Bush's term of office. However, economic conditions did not satisfy the common shorthand definition of recession, which is "a fall of a country's real gross domestic product in two or more successive quarters," and has led to some confusion about the procedure for determining the starting and ending dates of a recession.

The NBER's Business Cycle Dating Committee (BCDC) uses monthly, rather than quarterly, indicators to determine peaks and troughs in business activity,[4] as can be seen by noting that starting and ending dates are given by month and year, not quarters. However, controversy over the precise dates of the recession led to the characterization of the recession as the "Clinton Recession" by Republicans, if it could be traced to the final term of President Bill Clinton. BCDC members suggested they would be open to revisiting the dates of the recession as newer and more definitive data became available.[5] In early 2004, NBER President Martin Feldstein said:

> "It is clear that the revised data have made our original March date for the start of the recession much too late. We are still waiting for additional monthly data before making a final judgment. Until we have the additional data, we cannot make a decision."

However, the NBER has since confirmed that the recession started in March 2001.

From 2000 to 2001, the Federal Reserve, in a move to protect the economy from the overvalued stock market, made successive interest rate increases; while this may have initiated the readjustment, it is starkly contrasted with the severe, prolonged recession that would have occurred had the unsustainable growth continued unabated.[6] Using the stock market as an unofficial benchmark, a recession would have begun in March 2000 when the NASDAQ crashed following the collapse of the Dot-com bubble. The Dow Jones Industrial Average was

The Wreck of the Oglebay Norton

relatively unscathed by the NASDAQ's crash until the September 11, 2001 attacks, after which the DJIA suffered its worst one-day point loss and biggest one-week losses in history up to that point. The market rebounded, only to crash once more in the final two quarters of 2002. In the final three quarters of 2003, the market finally rebounded permanently, agreeing with the unemployment statistics that a recession defined in this way would have lasted from 2001 through 2003.

The Labor Department estimates that a net 1.735 million jobs were shed in 2001, with an additional net 508,000 lost during 2002. 2003 saw a small gain of a mere 105,000 jobs. Unemployment rose from 4.2% in February 2001 to 5.5% in November 2001, but did not peak until June 2003 at 6.3%, after which it declined to 5% by mid-2005.

Canada's economy is closely linked to that of the United States, and economic conditions south of the border tend to quickly make their way north. Canada's stock markets were especially hard hit by the collapse in high-tech stocks. For much of the 1990s the rapid rise of the TSX had almost wholly been attributed to two stocks: Nortel and BCE. Both companies were hard hit by the downturn, especially Nortel, which was forced to lay off much of its workforce. The events of September 11 also hurt the Canadian stock markets and were especially devastating to the already troubled airline sector.

Barr vs Lauer Lawsuites

Douglas N. Barr, Attorner and stockholder in Oglebay Norton, filed suite against John/ N. Lauer for 'Negligent Misrepresentation'. Lauer had stated

"Stick with me and in five years you'll have a billion dollar company and a$ 75 stock price."

The case went all the way to the Ohio Supreme Court, as detailed in http://www.sconet.state.oh.us/pdf_viewer/pdf_viewer.aspx?pdf=656967.pdf

Excerpts from the Ohio Supreme Court case:

June 6, 2009

IN THE SUPREME COURT OF OHIO
DOUGLAS N. BARR, Individually, And As
Trustee Of The Norton Family Trusts,
Plaintiff-Appellee,
V.
JOHN N. LAUER,
Defendant-Appellant.
On Appeal from the Cuyahoga County
Court of Appeals, Eighth Appellate
District, Case No. 08-092497
MEMORANDUM IN SUPPORT OF JURISDICTION
OF APPELLANT JOHN N. I.AUER

43

The Wreck of the Oglebay Norton

STATEMENT OF THE CASE AND FACTS

Plaintiff Douglas Barr was a shareholder of Oglebay Norton, both individually and as a trustee on behalf of various trusts. Barr alleges that some time in late 1997 he, along with co-trustee Robert I. Gale III, informed Oglebay's then-president of their desire to sell Barr's and the trusts' stock. *Barr v.* Lauer, 8th Dist. No. 92497, 2009-

Ohio-5563, at ¶3 (attached as Appendix A).

On December 17, 1997, at a meeting of the Oglebay Board of Directors, the Board of Directors passed a resolution authorizing (but not requiring) the repurchase of some or all of Barr's and the trusts' shares. Id.

Defendant John N. Lauer became Oglebay's new Chairman and CEO in 1998. On January 8, 1998, eight days after formally assuming the role of CEO, Lauer met with Barr and Gale. According to Barr, Lauer told him during that meeting:

"Stick with me and in five years you'll have a billion dollar company and a$ 75 stock price."

.

After Lauer made this statement, Barr, alleges, he decided not to sell the shares back to Oglebay.

Initially, Oglebay's stock rose with Lauer as the CEO. But the events of September ii, 2oot., coupled with the downturn in the steel industry, in Cleveland, hurt the company's performance. In February 2004, Oglebay filed for bankruptcy.,

Ten months later, Barr sued Lauer and six other former officers and directors of Oglebay. The trial court granted the defendants' motion to dismiss, and dismissal was affirmed as to all claims except the negligent misrepresentation claim against Lauer.

Barr v. Lauer, 8th Dist. No. 87514, 2007-Ohio-156. The trial court thereafter granted summary judgment on the remaining claim in favor of Lauer. Barr appealed the decision. Barr did not contend that the discovery rule applied. He told the trial court that]his is not ... a`discovery rnle' case," and did not argue the point on appeal. Nevertheless, the Eighth District reversed the grant of summary judgment, holding that the discovery rule applied to negligent misrepresentation claims and that factual questions existed as to whether the statute of limitations had run in this case..

Moreover, the Eighth District allowed a negligent misrepresentation claim based upon the phrase "stick with me and in five years you'll have a billion dollar company and a$75 stock price" to go forward without ever addressing the fact that forward-looking statements cannot form the basis of such a claim.

These holdings leave the Eighth District in conflict with other appellate courts in Ohio, with this Court's prior cases, as well as with hornbook law.

.CONCLUSION

For the foregoing reasons, this Court should hear this matter and reverse the decision below. The Court should not allow the Eighth District decision - which is in conflict with this Court's jurisprudence, the law of other jurisdictions, and the other appellate courts of Ohio - to stand.

JOHN N. LAUER SAILS ON

Despite the logical assumption that John N. Lauer's career went down with the ship in the Wreck Of The Oglebay Norton, he did not join the ranks of the unemployed.

John N. Lauer was appointed non-executive Chairman of the Board for Diebold, Incorporated, in December 2005. He is former chairman, president and chief executive officer of Oglebay Norton Company, Cleveland.

NORTH CANTON, Ohio, Jan. 21, 2013 /PRNewswire/ -- Diebold, Incorporated (NYSE:DBD) today announced that the company's Board of Directors has elected Henry D.G. Wallace as chairman of the board. . He replaces John N. Lauer, 73, whom the board will not be nominating for re-election to the board at the company's annual meeting of shareholders in April in accordance with the company's retirement policy. Lauer has held the non-executive chairman title since 2005 and has been a member of the company's board of directors since 1992.

John N. Lauer, May 2003: Retired Chairman of the Board, Oglebay Norton Co., Cleveland, Ohio (industrial minerals). Mr. Lauer will be retiring from the Diebold Board in2008.

John Lauer Director at Diebold

Total Annual Comp.: $337,380

Reported Accumulated Comp.: $961,029

About Diebold

Diebold, Incorporated is a global leader in providing integrated self-service delivery and security systems and services.

Diebold employs approximately 17,000 associates with representation in nearly 90 countries worldwide and is headquartered in the Canton, Ohio region, USA. Diebold is publicly traded on the New York Stock Exchange under the symbol 'DBD.' SOURCE Diebold, Incorporated

Oglebay Norton Historical

After 154 years, Oglebay Norton leaving Cleveland

By **Roger Mezger**
on February 14, 2008 at 10:17 AM, updated
February 14, 2008 at 7:59 PM

Oglebay Norton Co. Oglebay Norton's limestone quarries are concentrated in Michigan, such as this operation near Rogers City on the northern end of the state's Lower Peninsula.

• **Read the history of Oglebay Norton Co.**

Oglebay Norton Co, a fixture in Cleveland for 154 years, is closing its headquarters here as it merges into the North American operations of Belgian-owned Carmeuse Group.

Carmeuse will move about 50 people from Oglebay's Cleveland operations to Pittsburgh, where its **Carmeuse Lime & Stone** subsidiary is based, news reports from Pittsburgh said.

Carmeuse officials could not be reached, but **in a statement,** Thomas Buck, president and CEO of

Carmeuse Lime & Stone, said he welcomed Oglebay employees.

"The Oglebay acquisition brings Carmeuse significantly expanded reserves of high quality limestone, diverse markets and products, well positioned production facilities and a strong team of experienced people," he said.

Oglebay was formed in 1854 as a two-partner iron ore agency. The next year, John D. Rockefeller was hired, but he later quit in a pay dispute.

Oglebay owned the **Edmund Fitzgerald**, a freighter that sank in Lake Superior in 1975.

Carmeuse, a top lime producer, bought Oglebay in a deal it valued at $700 million, including debt. Carmeuse is North America's No. 1 producer of lime and needs a large supply of limestone for the kilns that produce it. Oglebay's rich quarries, concentrated around Lake Michigan, were a fit.

The agreement was struck after Oglebay adopted a poison pill to fend off a hostile takeover by a New York hedge fund, Harbinger Capital Partners. Harbinger offered $31 a share, while the Carmeuse purchase amounted to $36 a share.

Oglebay shares closed Thursday night at $35.98 in over-the-counter pink sheets trading Oglebay Chief

The Wreck of the Oglebay Norton

Executive Michael Lundin, Chief Financial Officer Julie Boland and Michael Minkel, senior vice president of operations, reportedly resigned as news of the finalized deal was released in Pittsburgh. A person answering the phone at Oglebay's offices in downtown Cleveland said Lundin no longer worked for the company.

He is in line to receive $4.7 million in severance and change-in-control awards, according to an Oglebay report to shareholders. The amount for Boland and Minkel is listed at $1.8 million each.

Oglebay's fortunes tumbled after Chief Executive John Lauer, a former Goodrich executive, took what he said was a narrowly focused company from a concentration on ore and shipping into new ventures – sand, specialty minerals and limestone. Calls to Lauer's office at Diebold Inc., where he is chairman, were not returned.

At first Oglebay's stock soared, topping $50 a share. But as the economy faltered, Oglebay, saddled with millions of dollars in debt, did too.

The great-granddaughter of Cleveland banker David Z. Norton, one of the company's scions, said the financial mess that led a once-bedrock company to

The Wreck of the Oglebay Norton

file for bankruptcy started when Oglebay lost its focus on Great Lakes shipping.

"It's very sad for Cleveland," said Carolyn Barr , whose father had a 60-year career at Oglebay. "The company was a huge employer for a long time, and over the years it just dwindled."

"My dad is spinning in his grave."

The Wreck of the Oglebay Norton

Oglebay Norton Corporation   From Wikipedia, the free encyclopedia

The **Oglebay Norton Corporation** operated ships on the Great Lakes. At one point their flagship was the SS Edmund Fitzgerald through their Columbia Transportation Division.

History The company's roots go back to 1851, when Hewitt & Tuttle, an iron ore brokerage, formed a shipping subsidiary.[1] after several mergers over the years, the firm became Oglebay, Norton in 1890, named for Earl Oglebay and David Z. Norton. The company was incorporated in 1924. Oglebay Norton was acquired by Carmeuse Lime & Stone, Inc. in 2008.

In 1858, an ambitious 18-year-old bookkeeper quit a small shipping firm here because his cash-strapped boss rejected his request for a $200 raise to $800 a year. The young man's name was John D. Rockefeller. That enterprise later became Oglebay Norton Co., a maker of industrial minerals and aggregates and an operator of a Great Lakes fleet.

The Wreck of the Oglebay Norton

OGLEBAY NORTON CO. - The Encyclopedia of Cleveland History

OGLEBAY NORTON CO., one of the oldest iron-ore houses in Cleveland, was established in 1851 as the firm of Hewitt & Tuttle. Cleveland commission agents Isaac Hewitt and Henry Tuttle received the first cargo of Lake Superior iron to reach Cleveland in 1852, and 2 years later they became agents for the Lake Superior Iron Co. Henry's son, Horace, developed a 3,000-acre tract on the Menominee range, and a new partnership was organized in 1884 when Wheeling, WV, industrialist EARL W. OGLEBAY† joined Horace A. Tuttle in Tuttle, Oglebay & Co. Upon the death of Horace Tuttle, Oglebay invited Cleveland banker DAVID Z. NORTON† to join him. In 1890 Oglebay Norton & Co. secured a contract to organize all of JOHN D. ROCKEFELLER†'s iron-ore properties in the Mesabi Range and to act as manager and sales agent. It acquired a fleet of 11 lake freighters, which became the Columbia Steamship Co. in 1921, later expanded and renamed the Columbia Transportation Co. in 1931. After its incorporation in 1924, the company branched into mining and selling coal, marketing fluorspar and ferro-alloys, and manufacturing insulation products for steel ingot pouring. During the 1930s it began to manage 4 docks along the Great Lakes.

The Wreck of the Oglebay Norton

As early as 1939, the firm, aware of the depletion of high-grade iron ores, initiated a study of low-grade minerals and established the Reserve Mining Co. to develop taconite. Its largest venture was the establishment of a huge taconite mine in Eveleth, MN, in the 1960s. In 1957 Oglebay Norton & Co. and its subsidiaries merged into a single unit, the Oglebay Norton Co., allowing for further growth and diversification into the areas of glass and foundry sand production and mining fracture sand for the petroleum industry. By the 1980s the company was earning more from nonsteel than from steel-related revenues. Subsequently, however, Oglebay Norton endeavored to focus on its primary business of Great Lakes shipping. In 1995 its Columbia Transportation division operated a fleet of 12 vessels. The main office was moved ca. 1988 from the Hanna Bldg. to the Diamond Bldg., 1100 Superior Ave., Cleveland.

The Wreck of the Oglebay Norton

Dec 02, 1999, 00:00 ET from Oglebay Norton Company

CLEVELAND, Dec. 2 /PRNewswire/ – Oglebay Norton Company (Nasdaq: OGLE)

today announced that it has completed the acquisition of the assets of

Franklin Industries' Mica business. The business consists of mining reserves

in North Carolina and New Mexico, production facilities, equipment and other

assets used in the mining, processing and distribution of mica.

John N. Lauer, Chairman, President and CEO of Oglebay Norton Company

reiterated: "This acquisition is an excellent strategic fit with our growth

and diversification plans into specialty minerals. The end-use markets for

mica are very compatible with the markets we currently serve in our other

segments."

He concluded: "Our vision is to become the most profitable growth company

in the industrial minerals arena and this acquisition meets our strategic

criteria for profitable growth in minerals."

The Wreck of the Oglebay Norton

Mica is a platy, flexible mineral used in a variety of industries to

enhance performance, such as building materials, plastics, lubricants, and

cosmetics.

Oglebay Norton Company, a Cleveland, Ohio-based company, provides

essential minerals to a broad range of markets, from building materials and

home improvement to the environmental, energy and metallurgical industries.

Building on a 145-year heritage, the company's vision is to become the premier

growth company in the industrial minerals industry. The company's website is

located at www.oglebaynorton.com .

Certain statements contained in this release are "forward-looking" in that

they reflect management's expectations and beliefs regarding a proposed

transaction. Forward-looking statements are necessarily subject to risks,

uncertainties and other factors, many of which are outside the control of the

Company, which could cause actual results to differ materially from such statements.

The Wreck of the Oglebay Norton

Oglebay Norton Signs Agreement to Acquire Global Stone Corporation

Accelerates Growth Strategy

Apr 15, 1998, 01:00 ET from Oglebay Norton Company announced today it has signed an agreement with Global Stone Corporation

(Toronto: GLS) of Oakville, Ontario, Canada pursuant to which Oglebay Norton

will make a tender offer for all the common shares o f Global Stone. Global

Stone is the fifth largest producer of lime in North A merica, and had net

revenues of Cdn. $151 million for the fiscal year end ed September 30, 1997.

Oglebay Norton's offer price for the Global Stone S hares will be

Cdn. $7.80 per share, payable in cash. There are ap proximately 32 million

common shares outstanding, including option shares . Oglebay Norton officials

said that it is anticipated that the bid will be mailed t o Global Stone's

shareholders on or before April 27, 1998. Completio n of the bid will be

subject to certain terms and conditions, including a minimum tender of two-thirds of the shares outstanding. Both companies no ted that the transaction

could be completed by May 31, 1998.

"We believe that Global Stone is an excellent strat egic fit, and advances

our stated desire to grow through selected value-add ed acquisitions," stated

John N. Lauer, Oglebay Norton's president and chief executive officer.

"The Acquisition of this well-managed company co mbined with our current

industrial sands operations and our pending acquisiti on of the Port Inland

limestone operations in Michigan, will make our indu strial minerals businesses

the largest single operating segment of Oglebay Nort on. We welcome warmly

the management and employees of Global Stone int o our company."

"Global Stone's strengths lie in its ownership of va st reserves of

limestone," said Robert R. Stone, Global Stone's Cha irman. "We are very

pleased to have the opportunity to join a company th at shares our core

qualities – excellent products, strong operating effici encies and exceptional

The Wreck of the Oglebay Norton

customer service – and has competent and motivated management. Global Stone

is excited about Oglebay's growth plans, and will bring additional

opportunities to achieve this strategy."

Global Stone will become a business unit of Oglebay Norton under

the continued direction of Global Stone's present senior management.

Global Stone's products, lime, chemical limestone and aggregate

stone, are used in a variety of manufacturing processes and industries,

including iron and steel, pulp and paper, chemical, environmental,

agricultural and construction. Global Stone has more than 700 employees, and

has eight operations in Canada and the United States.

Oglebay Norton is a Cleveland, Ohio-based company engaged in Great Lakes

marine transportation and material handling, and the mining and marketing of

industrial sands. In 1997 the company had revenues from continuing operations of $145 million.

The Wreck of the Oglebay Norton

The Edmund Fitzgerald was the Flagship of Oglebay Norton's Great Lakes fleet.

The Wreck of the Edmund Fitzgerald

Edmund Fitzgerald was an American Great Lakes freighter that sank in a Lake Superior storm on November 10, 1975, with the loss of the entire crew of 29. When launched on June 7, 1958, she was the largest ship on North America's Great Lakes, and she remains the largest to have sunk there.

For 17 years *Fitzgerald* carried taconite iron ore from mines near Duluth, Minnesota, to iron works in Detroit, Toledo, and other Great Lakes ports. As a "workhorse," she set seasonal haul records six times, often breaking her own previous record.[5][6] Captain Peter Pulcer was known for piping music day or night over the ship's intercom while passing through the St. Clair and Detroit Rivers (between Lakes Huron and Erie), and entertaining spectators at the Soo Locks (between Lakes Superior and Huron) with a running commentary about the ship.[5] Her size, record-breaking performance, and "DJ captain" endeared *Fitzgerald* to boat watchers.[7]

The Wreck of the Oglebay Norton

Carrying a full cargo of ore pellets with Captain Ernest M. McSorley in command, she embarked on her ill-fated voyage from Superior, Wisconsin, near Duluth, on the afternoon of November 9, 1975. En route to a steel mill near Detroit, *Fitzgerald* joined a second freighter, SS *Arthur M. Anderson*. By the next day, the two ships were caught in a severe storm on Lake Superior, with near <u>hurricane-force</u> winds and waves up to 35 feet (11 m) high. Shortly after 7:10 p.m., *Fitzgerald* suddenly sank in Canadian (Ontario) waters 530 feet (160 m) deep, about 17 miles (15 nautical miles; 27 kilometers) from Whitefish Bay near the twin cities of Sault Ste. Marie, Michigan, and Sault Ste. Marie, Ontario—a distance *Fitzgerald* could have covered in just over an hour at her top speed. Although *Fitzgerald* had reported being in difficulty earlier, no distress signals were sent before she sank; Captain McSorley's last message to *Anderson* said, "We are holding our own." Her crew of 29 perished, and no bodies were recovered. The exact cause of the sinking remains unknown, though many books, studies, and expeditions have examined it. *Fitzgerald* might have fallen victim to the high waves of the storm, suffered structural failure, been swamped with water entering through her cargo hatches or deck, experienced topside damage, or shoaled in a shallow part of Lake Superior.

The Wreck of the Oglebay Norton

The disaster is one of the best-known in the history of Great Lakes shipping. Gordon Lightfoot made it the subject of his 1976 hit song "The Wreck of the *Edmund Fitzgerald*" after reading an article, "The Cruelest Month", in the November 24, 1975, issue of *Newsweek*. The sinking led to changes in Great Lakes shipping regulations and practices that included mandatory survival suits, depth finders, positioning systems, increased freeboard

GORDON LIGHTFOOT LYRICS
"The Wreck Of The Edmund Fitzgerald"

The legend lives on from the Chippewa on down
Of the big lake they call Gitche Gumee
The lake, it is said, never gives up her dead
When the skies of November turn gloomy
With a load of iron ore twenty-six thousand tons more
Than the Edmund Fitzgerald weighed empty
[Former version:] That good ship and true was a bone to be chewed
[Latter version:] That good ship and crew was a bone to be chewed
When the gales of November came early

The ship was the pride of the American side
Coming back from some mill in Wisconsin
As the big freighters go, it was bigger than most
With a crew and good captain well seasoned
Concluding some terms with a couple of steel firms
When they left fully loaded for Cleveland

The Wreck of the Oglebay Norton

Then later that night when the ship's bell rang
Could it be the north wind they'd been feelin'?

The wind in the wires made a tattle-tale sound
When the wave broke over the railing
And every man knew, as the captain did too
'Twas the witch of November come stealin'
The dawn came late and the breakfast had to wait
When the gales of November came slashin'
When afternoon came it was freezing rain
In the face of a hurricane west wind

When suppertime came, the old cook came on deck
Saying, "Fellas, it's too rough to feed ya."
[Former version:] At seven PM a main hatchway
caved in
[Latter version:] At seven PM it grew dark, it was then
He said, "Fellas, it's been good to know ya."
The captain wired in he had water comin' in
And the good ship and crew was in peril
And later that night when his lights went out of sight
Came the wreck of the Edmund Fitzgerald

Does anyone know where the love of God goes
When the waves turn the minutes to hours?
The searchers all say they'd have made Whitefish Bay
If they'd put fifteen more miles behind her
They might have split up or they might have capsized
They may have broke deep and took water
And all that remains is the faces and the names
Of the wives and the sons and the daughters

The Wreck of the Oglebay Norton

Lake Huron rolls, Superior sings
In the rooms of her ice-water mansion
Old Michigan steams like a young man's dreams
The islands and bays are for sportsmen
And farther below, Lake Ontario
Takes in what Lake Erie can send her
And the iron boats go as the mariners all know
With the gales of November remembered

[Former version:] In a musty old hall in Detroit they
prayed
[Latter version:] In a rustic old hall in Detroit they
prayed
In the Maritime Sailors' Cathedral
The church bell chimed 'til it rang twenty-nine times
For each man on the Edmund Fitzgerald
The legend lives on from the Chippewa on down
Of the big lake they call Gitche Gumee
Superior, they said, never gives up her dead
When the gales of November come early .

The Wreck of the Oglebay Norton

The Wreck of the Oglebay Norton

Ship MV Oglebay Norton history

American Integrity - BoatNerd.Com

by George Wharton

This Great Lakes self unloading bulk carrier was built in two sections as hull #717 by Bay Shipbuilding and Dry Dock co., Sturgeon Bay, WI. The keel for the 660' bow section was laid on October 6, 1976 and was launched April 28, 1977. The completed "super carrier" was launched June 6, 1978 as the Lewis Wilson Foy for her new owners Bethlehem Steel Corp., Great Lakes Steamship Division, Cleveland, OH. Of note, the vessel was originally slated to be named Burns Harbor but was changed before/during construction.

The vessel is powered by 4 GM Electro-Motive Division 20-645-E7 V-20 cylinder two stroke cycle, single acting 3,600 b.h.p diesel engines burning marine diesel oil. The power is fed through Falk single reduction gears to 2 controllable pitch propellers giving the vessel a service speed of 18.4 m.p.h. She is equipped with both bow and stern thrusters. The vessel's 37 hatches feed into 7 holds where she is capable of carrying 78,850 tons at her mid summer draft of 34'00". Her self unloading system feeds a stern mounted 250' discharge boom that can be swung 92 degrees to port or starboard and unload at a rate of up to 8,930 tons (10,000 net tons) per hour.

The Wreck of the Oglebay Norton

The Lewis Wilson Foy departed Sturgeon Bay June 8, 1978 on her maiden voyage in ballast to Superior, WI where 57,952 tons of iron ore pellets were loaded on board destined for Burns Harbor, IN. The taconite pellet trade from Lake Superior ports to Bethlehem Steel's lower Lake Michigan facilities were the focus of the vessel's activities in her early years. The vessel sustained some hull damage after hitting an underwater obstruction in June, 1979. On September 15, 1981; the Lewis Wilson Foy was in collision with Algoma's E. B. Barber receiving three holes in her side. Then, on July 6, 1982; the vessel struck the breakwall and grounded at Taconite Harbor, MN. The bulk carrier had three flooded tanks and was listing; sustaining $2.5 million in damages to her propellers, shafts, rudders, and hull plates. She arrived at Sturgeon Bay on July 12, 1982 for repairs. The Lewis Wilson Foy loaded a record 69,701 tons of ore at Escanaba, MI for Inland Steel at Indiana Harbor. This record was followed up with a Great Lakes record of 72,351 tons of ore loaded at Escanaba on November 26, 1986 also bound for Indiana Harbor. This record was possible partially due to the record high water levels on the Great Lakes that season.

On July 16, 1990; Bethlehem Steel entered into an agreement to sell the bulk carrier to Columbia Transportation Division, Oglebay Norton Co., Cleveland, OH with the deal being finalized in December of that year. The vessel was officially renamed **Oglebay Norton** at a board of directors meeting on February 28, 1991 and began sailing under her new banner at the beginning of the 1991

The Wreck of the Oglebay Norton

season. The Oglebay Norton became the 2nd "super carrier" sailing in the Columbia fleet; the other vessel being the Columbia Star. The new member of the fleet was named to honor the Oglebay Norton Company. With the phasing out of the Columbia Transportation Division in 1994, the vessel came under the direct ownership of Oglebay Norton Co. with a resulting change in the paint scheme of her stacks (the 5-pointed star with the "C" replaced with a 4-pointed star with "ON") and a new corporate logo appearing below her name on her bow.

A reflection of different cargoes now being carried, the Oglebay Norton set a limestone record in 1992 when she loaded 52,749 tons of the product. On April 26, 1998; the Oglebay Norton blew hydraulic lines while downbound in the St. Marys River system affecting the steering of the vessel. After a soft grounding and repairs, she was able to proceed with no further damage. Then, on August 24, 1999; a port steering pump failure resulted in the Oglebay Norton mooring at the St. Clair (Edison) power plant on the St. Clair River for repairs. The vessel was upbound in ballast on the St. Clair River when the incident occurred. The end of August, 2000 saw the retirement of her Master, Capt. Constantine (Gus) Markakis after sailing for Oglebay Norton for 28 years.

The Oglebay Norton is now owned by Oglebay Norton Marine Services Co., LLC; a division of Oglebay Norton Co. In January of 2002, Oglebay Norton Marine and

The Wreck of the Oglebay Norton

American Steamship Co. pooled their fleet operations under the United Shipping Alliance, LLC name with both partner companies retaining ownership of their individual assets. The Oglebay Norton's trade routes are now focused on western coal from Lake Superior ports to power plants at Monroe and St. Clair, MI; supplemented with loads of taconite pellets.

On June 6, 2006 in a joint announcement made with American Steamship Co. of Williamsville, NY, Oglebay Norton Co. announced the sale of the Oglebay Norton and five of her fleetmates to American Steamship Co. (ASC) for $120 million. With the sale came a new name: **American Integrity**. The other vessels going to ASC were the Armco, Columbia Star, Courtney Burton, Fred R. White Jr. and Middletown.

100 Years of Oglebay Norton

100 Years of Oglebay Norton

A booklet published in 1954

Note: This book scanned from the book published in 1954, 63 years ago. Images are enhanced as much as possible.

"Oglebay, Norton"

100 Years on the Great Lakes

HARRIE S. TAYLOR

100 Years of Oglebay Norton

*"Were American Newcomen to do naught else, our
work is well done if we succeed in sharing with
America a strengthened inspiration to continue
the struggle towards a nobler Civilization—
through wider knowledge and understanding of the
hopes, ambitions, and deeds of leaders in the past
who have upheld Civilization's material progress.
As we look backward, let us look forward."*

—CHARLES PENROSE
*Senior Vice-President for North America
The Newcomen Society of England*

*This statement, crystallizing a broad purpose of the society, was first read
at the Newcomen Meeting at New York World's Fair on August 5, 1939,
when American Newcomen were guests of The British Government*

"Actorum Memores simul affectamus Agenda"

100 Years of Oglebay Norton

AMERICAN NEWCOMEN, *through the years, has honored numerous corporate enterprises in many paths of human endeavor, and both in the United States of America and in Canada; and has honored the memories of leaders whose vision, courage, determination, resourcefulness, hard work, and abiding Faith created these enterprises and carried them forward. Such a Newcomen manuscript is this, celebrating the 100th Anniversary (1854-1954) of an organization of foremost standing in American Business: Oglebay, Norton and Company.*

᪅ ᪅

100 Years of Oglebay Norton

THE CENTENARY *which this Newcomen Address cele-brated, of one of America's highly respected industrial enterprises, gave happy opportunity for The Newcomen Society in North America to pay respect to* ROBERT C. NORTON, *Chairman of the Board of Oglebay, Norton and Company, a Vice-Chairman and one of the charter members of the Cleveland Committee in this Society. Mr. Norton typifies the best of American business and industrial leadership and traditions—as does the long-established organization at which*

he is the head.

ଙ   ଙ

"Oglebay, Norton"

100 Years on the Great Lakes

HARRIE S. TAYLOR

MEMBER OF THE NEWCOMEN SOCIETY
PRESIDENT
OGLEBAY, NORTON AND COMPANY
CLEVELAND
OHIO

100 Years of Oglebay Norton

*This Newcomen Address, dealing with the
history of Oglebay, Norton and Company and
celebrating the 100th Anniversary (1854-1954)
of that organization, was delivered at the
"1954 Cleveland Dinner" of The Newcomen*

100 Years of Oglebay Norton

INTRODUCTION OF MR. TAYLOR, AT CLEVELAND ON
MAY 11, 1954, BY CHARLES R. HOOK, CHAIRMAN OF
THE BOARD, ARMCO STEEL CORPORATION, MIDDLETOWN,
OHIO; VICE-CHAIRMAN OF THE CINCINNATI COMMIT-
TEE, IN THE NEWCOMEN SOCIETY IN NORTH AMERICA.

My fellow members of Newcomen:

I T IS a great source of satisfaction to me to make this introduction:—not only as a member of Newcomen, or because of the
years of business association with the company we are honor-
ing tonight—but through genuine friendship of long standing with
the men of Oglebay, Norton and Company. Of the close relation-
ships I have had in business, none has provided me with any
greater pleasure.

❦ ❦

Around the turn of the Century, in the early days of our corporation, we purchased pig iron from the Columbus Iron and Steel
Company who in turn received iron ore from Oglebay, Norton and
Company. Later, in 1917, Columbus Iron and Steel became a part
of our organization which at that time was "The American Rolling
Mill Company." So you can see that directly or indirectly we have
shared the experiences of our honored guests for over half of their
one hundred years.

We have seen this company spread its wings in its second half
century, broadening from the sale and mining of iron ore to its

[5]

76

present management and sales for many operating companies with diverse products and services.

We have seen the courage, vision, and business integrity of the founders carried on by succeeding generations of management. This firmly entrenched heritage has enabled this company and its people to enjoy an enviable business life.

❧ ❧

Earl W. Oglebay and David Z. Norton, founders of the present corporate name, risked capital and secure position but ultimately provided a solid business foundation for the firm. Mr. Oglebay, who granted famous Oglebay Park to the City of Wheeling, West Virginia, was a wholesale commission merchant. He foresaw in the early 1880's the tremendous growth possibilities of the budding iron ore industry. David Z. Norton, a well-known Cleveland banker, joined Mr. Oglebay in 1890, bringing with him a contract for the sale of ore produced at the many mines of The Lake Superior Consolidated Mines Co. owned by his friend —John D. Rockefeller. Both men passed away in the 'mid-twenties after many successful years and great contributions to our industrial development.

❧ ❧

The partnership of Oglebay, Norton and Company was changed to a corporation in 1924, at which time the second generation took over the reins of the fast-growing company.

Crispin Oglebay was appointed President and remained in that position until his death in 1949. He was nationally known as a business leader, philanthropist, and sportsman. Our honored guest, Robert C. Norton, presently Chairman of the Board, also became an officer at the time of incorporation. A few years later his brother, Laurence H. Norton, became an officer and director. These two brothers have made admirable contributions to our present industrial and social climate.

❧ ❧

Another good friend of mine in this organization is Courtney Burton, grandson of E. W. Oglebay. He is a Vice-President of

[6]

100 Years of Oglebay Norton

Oglebay, Norton and Company, president and director of several companies, and active in many cultural, civic, and other organizations.

Another grandson of a founder who carries on tradition is Fred R. White, Jr., nephew of the Nortons, who is Vice-President in charge of Vessel Operations.

These energetic young men have the same devotion to duty, the same vision and sense of responsibility as their forebears.

I would also like to mention the name of E. W. Sloan, Jr. their very capable Vice-President and Treasurer.

ꙮ ꙮ

Our speaker tonight is Harrie S. Taylor, President of this honored company. He is a native of Chautauqua, New York, and received his advanced academic education at Allegheny College in Pennsylvania. Later he received a law degree from Western Reserve University Law School. As happened to many, Mr. Taylor's education was interrupted by the First World War when he served in France as an officer with the 15th Field Artillery in balloon observation. He was admitted to the Ohio Bar in 1921 and became associated with the Nation's most noted admiralty law firm, Goulder, White, and Garry. In 1936, after many years practical experience, he was appointed General Counsel of Oglebay, Norton and Company, and in 1949 was promoted to the presidency. In addition to this major responsibility, he holds many executive positions and directorships with organizations identified with mining and Great Lakes commerce.

He is a man with great zeal and enthusiasm for the Great Lakes Region and its economic importance to this great nation of ours. He has made valuable contributions to the industries of this region with particular devotion of time in the last decade to the development of the all-important taconite ores of the Mesabi Range.

ꙮ ꙮ

It gives me great pleasure to present to you an honored guest and a brother in Newcomen: HARRIE S. TAYLOR.

ꙮ ꙮ

100 Years of Oglebay Norton

My fellow members of Newcomen:

C OULDN'T be a nicer thing happen to a man—that I can think of—than to be actually invited to talk shop—that is to talk about our own firm which is being so highly honored tonight by The Newcomen Society in North America and you distinguished gentlemen assembled here. It is worth waiting a hundred years for a thing like that. I said our firm— but I mean Henry Tuttle's—he started it—hundred years ago.

❦ ❦

Now here I stand, *Mr. Chairman*, to speak for Henry Tuttle, and I don't even know what he would think of me. Don't know if he'd even hire me. If he could edit my manuscript—or if he *is* editing my manuscript—I don't know what he's thinking of it. I'd want him to like it.

But I have an idea how he'd instruct me. He was a salesman after all. I think he'd say: "Harrie Taylor, time is short. Don't waste it tonight." And he was a rugged, fundamental kind of thinker. I think he'd say: "Harrie Taylor, if you have all those very considerable men willing to listen, have the grace to stick to

[8]

fundamentals. And if you're going into 100 years of history, remember there's only one excuse for history—explain the past to improve the future."

❧ ❧

That's a presumptuous objective for a speaker. But if I don't attempt it, what good am I to you? And if I don't attempt it—what will Henry Tuttle say to me—when we meet?

In my effort to get to basics I'm not going to start a hundred years ago. I'd like to start with this *pan*—and work back from it.

In a way, it's the sum and summary of 100 years on the Great Lakes. And it's very fundamental indeed. It's a two-quart pan. $6.45. Extruded, 16 gauge stainless. Belongs to Mrs. Taylor. It's out of keeping with the silver service and white linen here. But I don't think it will offend any man in *this* room.

You see, the great and wonderful thing about this pan—to me —in fact to *us*—is that Mrs. Taylor doesn't like it. Neither does Mrs. Higgins, Mrs. Jones, and Mrs. Smith. It's the best pan money can buy of its type—the very best. But Mrs. Higgins is dissatisfied with it. It's three days old—and already—it's not good enough.

I don't know who made this pan. But I'm willing to bet they already know they're going to have to make a better one. I dare say there's a sales manager somewhere having a big argument with a production manager and a designer this week. The old dies are still good but they will have to be scrapped.

They're probably mad, unhappy, frustrated!

But it's a good thing for all of us that Mrs. Higgins is dissatisfied with this pan. A hundred years ago her great grandmother also was dissatisfied with the things she had to work with. That's what put old Henry Tuttle in business—that plus the presence of that body of water out there 4 blocks from this building. To explain that I'll have to go back to a little group of determined men.

❧ ❧

For the beginnings with which we are concerned have to do with men. They have been called men of wisdom and courage and

[9]

vision; but those are polite clichés that don't begin to do justice
to the kind of men these were. Better we should describe them,
I think, as hard-headed, tough-minded, square-jawed fortune
hunters. If they built empires for future generations, that was
all right. But first off, they wanted to make money. These were
men used to weighing the risks, willing to pay the price; if they
lost there'd be no whimpering; if they won they'd press their
advantage. In short, they were men of enterprise who understood
about Mrs. Higgins' cooking pan—and it's no wonder they built
America.

🙟 🙟

They were gathered in the Autumn of 1846 in the tap room of
the Weddell House right over here on West 6th Street in Cleveland—where the barber shop is now. They were there at that
time because a man named J. Lang Cassels, age 38, had just come
back from the Michigan Peninsula and the Lake Superior Country.
They had sent him up there on an errand. Now he was back. And
what he had to say was disappointing.

They had sent him up there to find silver—possibly even gold
—at least copper.

And what did he bring back? Nothing.

Oh—he brought back a handful of *iron ore*. Talked about how
he'd found mountains of this material. Had a lot to say about how
it was close to Lake Superior. How conceivably it could be brought
down here. How if the coal could be brought up from the South,
the Lake Erie cities would be planked squarely across the cross-
road of fortune.

But even as he spoke, the Doctor could see that most of the
men in the room were not listening. Some were already leaving.
They had sent him for gold. He brought them iron ore. Some
half a century later Andrew Carnegie was to straighten out his
previous wrong judgment with his often-quoted remark: "Gold
is precious but iron ore is priceless." And even Carnegie learned
that the hard way. But there in the tap room of the Weddell
House in the Year 18 and 46, iron ore 800 miles away seemed
worthless.

[10]

One by one the men began to leave the room, presumably to seek more practical fortunes. There was iron enough in Ohio to last a generation, they said, and they wanted profits before that. But a few men stayed for they had caught the good doctor's excitement. Samuel L. Mather was there and so were Isaac and Morgan Hewitt. They talked long into the night. There was enough iron ore right in Ohio to last a hundred years—at the current rate of consumption. But it was low grade kidney and blackband and it was running thin.

There were a few there, too, who knew the going price of iron kettles, each of which was costing Mrs. Higgins five days of her husband's work-week.

❦ ❦

Sure, we had ore in Ohio. But not much of it, and the competition for it by the Hanging Rock iron masters down near Ironton, Ohio—made it unlikely that Mrs. Higgins would get a better kettle very soon, or for any less money.

Unless—well, a small caucus of men in the Weddell House tap room sat down to calculate the risks of bringing iron ore out of the Lake Superior Country to make a kettle for Mrs. Higgins.

❦ ❦

First the ore had to be transported some 12 miles from the iron mountain to the Lake Superior shore. That meant a road, eventually a railroad. Then the heavy material would have to be loaded into some kind of ship—at that moment there wasn't much in the way of sailing vessels on Lake Superior. At Sault Ste. Marie, the ore would have to be transferred from the ship to wagons, to be transported around the Falls. Then it would have to be loaded again onto a vessel which would carry it to Cleveland. Where it would again have to be handled. That wouldn't make very many kettles very fast. So only men who were sure that we were going to use an awful lot of kettles—that is Civilization—would have given such a project a second thought. But a few such men were gathered this night.

100 Years of Oglebay Norton

The first and biggest obstacle was that portage around the Falls at the Soo. Nothing much could be accomplished until a vessel could be loaded in the upper reaches of Superior and unloaded on the South shore of Lake Erie. Thus began the drama of the Soo Canal.

When they asked Uncle Sam for help, Henry Clay opposed it, saying: "This is a project beyond the moon." But Clay didn't understand about iron kettles and there was much sympathy with his point of view. But the iron men, having set the wheels in motion, didn't wait for their canal. Several iron mining companies were formed, among them one called the Cleveland Iron Mining Company.

The first shipment of ore to the lower lakes was made in 1852, comprising six barrels. It was dug by hand, hauled by mule team to water, hauled by mule again around the Falls, wheelbarrowed onto a sailing ship, and, legend has it, it was eventually consigned to the commission firm of Hewitt and Tuttle.

Now working this way—they managed to bring down a thousand tons in 12 months. But income from that small tonnage didn't pay for the hay the mules ate the winter before. But it accomplished its purpose nevertheless. The lower lakes iron masters were soon clamoring for more upper lakes ore and when Mrs. Higgins got the idea that her better cooking pan was somehow involved, she spoke right up—and when Mrs. Higgins speaks— she's heard!

So, in the Year 1855, a new day came for the iron men, for Cleveland, and for the world—and for Mrs. Higgins, most of all. The canal was born. The two-masted Brig *Columbia*, in that year, locked through the new Soo Canal with a deckful of 132 tons of the reddest ore a down-lakes furnace master had ever shoveled.

It had come from the place Henry Clay called "the land beyond the moon." And Henry Clay died that year.

❦ ❦

Seven thousand tons of ore came down the next year and Hewitt and Tuttle handled most of it. Business was so brisk the firm had

[12]

83

to put on an extra clerk and bookkeeping assistant. A bright-eyed sixteen-year-old boy was found for the job. No one was impressed, just then, that his name was John D. Rockefeller.

And now the talk in the Weddell House was excited and fast. You'd hear the conflicting gossip, and you'd have to make up your own mind:

You'd hear that old Iron John Campbell had iron piled six pigs high and a mile long on the Ohio River and couldn't sell it for love nor money. But up on the lakes it was just the opposite—everybody had iron fever.

You'd hear that Samuel L. Mather was reaching to the north country to fetch down more ore in sailships, while some others were building a steam vessel to beat him to it. Same time the Mackin Brothers were trying to steal the rail iron market from the British.

You'd hear that stock prices in the new upper lakes mining companies were too high. Then you'd hear: "Mister, a hundred dollars a share is dirt cheap when you figure Hewitt's already brought down four loads of merchantable ore out of the Lake Superior District. Don't come around next week with your money. You'll be too late."

And down on the docks you'd hear one say: "As long as they're unloadin' this red stuff they'll need me and me mules." And the answer: "Don't be too sure. I hear there is steam donkey that empties a hull in three days."

Yes, the iron fever became an epidemic along the lakes, and a central figure in the drama is Henry Tuttle, ore merchant.

In 1861, having left Hewitt, he becomes a partner in the Lake Superior Iron Company—so he is now not just a broker of other people's ore—he has some of his own to sell. No one notices that John Rockefeller, the bookkeeper, gives up his job to go into business for himself.

About this time, too, down in Wheeling, West Virginia, Crispin Oglebay, a banker and merchant, decides there is a considerable future in iron and becomes interested in the Benwood Iron Works.

[13]

100 Years of Oglebay Norton

By the late 1860's, Henry Tuttle's sons have come of age and he takes them into his firm which becomes H. B. Tuttle and Company.

Now while all this was going on—you'd hear more gossip up on Euclid Avenue.

How Henry Chisholm's rails began coming back on him. The rolling floor boss complained that he had to re-roll the rails. And Henry said: "Don't reroll 'em. From now on they'll all come back on us."

"But these were all inspected!"

"Sure they were all inspected. Our rails are the same as always—the Country's changing. We've made our last iron rail. Steel is the thing."

❦ ❦

And that brings us to a landmark. Because when the time came that Mrs. Higgins had to have a better kettle and railroaders had to have different rails—the iron men went out and brought back to this town the third Bessemer converter in the Country.

The Bessemer converter ushered in the age of steel—which cut the price of rails and cooking pans so that we needed more ore. To meet the need Henry Tuttle chartered a few more ships to carry ore, exclusively. And in evidence of his faith in Mrs. Higgins' continuing dissatisfaction he went out and invested in ore properties himself.

❦ ❦

So in 1869—650,000 tons of ore shipped down the lakes. By 1880, it had become a torrent of 1,950,000 tons; by 1890, a deluge —9 million tons.

❦ ❦

That brings me to the part of this story that makes it worth the telling. As I've been speaking, I imagine many of you have been saying to yourselves, "What about the Mathers, the Hannas, the Elys, the Browns, the Wades, and how about Peter White —and all the other pioneers of the trade?" Let me assure you that no one knows better than I that the tremendous accomplishments of these times were the work of many men and many, many

[14]

companies. There was rivalry among them; bitter fighting, in fact —but there was also teamwork of a high order. The problems, after all, were common to all of them, and any man or organization who could help solve them soon found a welcome place at a kind of iron round-table whose foundations were laid in those early years and which has held together even to this day.

🐝 🐝

With the coming of steel, the industrial horizons began moving outward. Until then blast furnaces were small affairs, twenty-five feet high with a daily capacity of some five tons. But within the decade from 1870 to 1880 the picture changed. Furnaces began to take on the lines they have today. Spurred by the introduction of Connellsville coking coal, daily capacities jumped to a hundred tons, and the United States of America assumed world leadership in the production of iron.

🐝 🐝

In 1886, the Otis Steel Company of Cleveland built the first successful open hearth furnace. Despite its advantages, it wasn't until 1910 that open-hearth steel caught up with Bessemer steel. In that year tonnages by the two methods were about equal.

🐝 🐝

Meanwhile men began to specialize. New and better rolling equipment was built and there began to be specialists in the production of plates, sheets, tubes, wire, and strip. And as steel expanded so did the economy.

Mrs. Higgins now had a cooking pan she could lift with one hand, she was pleased with it, but now she wanted two pans for two different uses.

In the middle of all these changes and taking active part in them was the firm Henry Tuttle had founded. Henry died in 1878, but his sons Horace and Frederick carried on the business.

Partners came and went during these turbulent, transition years; but, in 1884, the Oglebays re-entered the scene to begin a new era.

[15]

100 Years of Oglebay Norton

Earl Oglebay inherited his father's interests in the Benwood and other iron works and one day decided to follow the iron industry back to its source. On a trip to the upper lakes he became fascinated with the ore business and bought an interest in an ore mine in what was already known as the Gogebic Range in Michigan and Wisconsin. Then he came back to Cleveland to look up Horace Tuttle. A few months later they were doing business as Tuttle, Oglebay and Company.

It seemed to both the partners that between the ore interests and the steel interests the chief and most important component they could supply—was coordination.

Their principal job, to help bring the elements of steelmaking together so the Nation could get on with its destiny.

❦ ❦

Horace Tuttle, having lent his vision and organizing genius to this new concept, suddenly departed from the scene, killed in a railroad accident on a trip to the iron ranges in 1889. Oglebay then bought the interests of the Tuttle heirs and a great name disappeared from our story.

❦ ❦

And then along came another ground-thumping change. For 120 miles along the north shore of Lake Superior, starting at a place called Mesaba, they found you could almost scuff the pine needles aside and you were practically standing on red dust that ran 60 percent iron dried. The great new Mesabi Range opened —and brought back an old acquaintance to the iron trade.

❦ ❦

John Rockefeller had been getting by all right on his own— outside of the iron business. Something about oil. In fact he probably wouldn't know blackband ore from Mesabi. But one thing he had learned in the oil business that he thought applied to any business—the importance of controlling your sources.

He thought the steel industry would one day discover the importance of owning its own ore sources, and when that day came— well, they'd have to come talk to him.

[16]

100 Years of Oglebay Norton

Rockefeller acquired the interests of the famed Merritt Brothers who had pioneered the Mesabi Range. That gave him the world's richest ore field. To supervise the marketing of it, he called on an old friend, David Z. Norton. He told the father of the present Chairman of our Board, R. C. Norton, to find a suitable partner for this enterprise. Thus, at long last, the firm Oglebay, Norton comes on the scene.

They had plenty of ore, but ore alone has never been enough. The trick then was to dump it over the side along the lower lakes docks for something like $2.00 a ton.

That meant ships. And Rockefeller meant to have the best.

Knowing nothing about the business, he called in a fellow Clevelander—Sam Mather—son of Sam L. "How would you like to superintend the building for me of two dozen all-steel ore boats —as large as the channels will float?"

Mr. Mather was perhaps taken back. But being in the iron trade, he said: "Why sure. When do you want them?"

Now there were only 12 ship builders on the lakes. So if Mather had announced that he planned to build 2 dozen ships, Mr. Rockefeller would have to pay through the nose—which he was known to dislike. Sam Mather went about the job systematically. He let it be known that he was accepting competitive bids on one or two ships.

The day before final orders were let, men representing 40 years of shipbuilding assembled in Mr. Mather's outer office. They had seen lean times and they had bid tight. One by one they were called in and each came out smiling. Each went to the Weddell tap room to celebrate victory—and sympathize with his competitors. To their surprise each had received a similar slip awarding contracts to the capacities of their yards. They had a good laugh all around—it says here—and set to work building the greatest and most important fleet in history.

❧ ❧

By 1901, Rockefeller had 60 ships, including the first 500-footer. Now John D. leaves us—when he sold his ore lands and control of the Bessemer fleet to J. P. Morgan's U. S. Steel—what we have come to call The Corporation.

❦ ❦

In looking at the Great Lakes business it appears to be a triangle, namely: raw materials, vessel transportation, and docks.

One side of this triangle is always out of balance—and the effort to even them up—is what brings Mrs. Higgins better pans.

By the 1870's, the iron men had built a vast machine extending from the Lake Superior mines to the Erie docks. Most of it was working well.

But at the unloading docks the machine broke down. When a ship made port every able-bodied man grabbed a shovel. First the ore was shoveled onto a staging in the hold, then from the stage to the deck, then to wheelbarrows which were pushed along a catwalk to the dock. In a week you could unload 300 tons. At that rate, the ships were spending more time at the docks than on the lakes—and when the ships don't move, nothing moves.

The wheelbarrows were holding up America!

❦ ❦

That's how it was when A. E. Brown, fresh from engineering school, came down to the docks to deliver a message from his father, who was Fayette Brown, one of the early iron men.

Young Alex had a message for a ship's captain, but he had to wait until the captain got through profanely conferring with the dock foreman. The captain was suggesting: "Blast it, Mr. Sommers, must I wait until my bloomin' hull rots off to get this ship under way! Four days now your men are swarming over her like mosquitoes and I don't see that you've moved any of the dirty stuff."

Young Alex Brown broke in. "Mr. Sommers," he said, "why not rig a block and tackle to the mast. You could shovel ore into a bucket, hitch a horse to the load and hoist it out."

Well, no one had much faith in the idea, but young Brown took off his coat and went to work on it to cut unloading time in half. After that the docks crawled with horses from Lorain to Conneaut.

[18]

However, the ship-builders undid this work by building bigger hulls.

❦ ❦

A few years later, in Cleveland a portable steam engine rigged with a mast, cable, windlass, and scoop was developed. It replaced many of the men, all of the horses, and it unloaded 400 tons from the Ship *Massillon* in one single day.

Ore tonnages leaped.

❦ ❦

Now for years a man named George Hulett had been interested in the see-saw drama of the ore unloaders. In 1899, he decided to play a part in it himself.

He called together a group of engineers. "Gentlemen," he said, "I propose to build the biggest post-hole digger in the history of the world. You are all familiar with the principle. The digger jams into the ground, you pull the handles to close the jaws and lift out the soil. We're going to apply that principle to unloading ore. We'll unload ships that way."

If anyone but George Hulett had proposed it, chances are he'd have been laughed off the lake front. But a few years after he had outlined the principle to his staff, there was a strange-looking arm in the sky along the docks at Conneaut, Ohio, Hulett's birthplace.

At Hulett's signal the huge arm began to bend at the elbow. Slowly it began to descend. The fingers closed and the arm drew back. Andrew Carnegie's mouth opened as the hand withdrew from the hull and dropped ten tons of ore into a railroad car. In five hours the vessel was unloaded. And the price of cooking pans dropped a quarter of a dollar.

❦ ❦

And we at Oglebay Norton, along with our associated companies, are proud to help carry on this race in operation of improved dock facilities at Lake Erie ports, and fleet operations.

Speed and careful handling are the keynotes of today's coal loading and ore unloading business. Modern coal car dumpers have the capacity to load a car of coal a minute, lifting it high in the air and dumping it gently into the holds of vessels. Ore docks with the latest equipment are able to unload 20,000 ton vessels in a matter of a few hours.

ᵜ ᵜ

Vessels also enter the loading and unloading picture. In the constant effort to keep the ships moving—and as independent as possible from shore side bottlenecks—where equipment is not available—the self unloader was built. Here is a vessel which has to be loaded by shore facilities—but with cargo once aboard, she can move into nearly any reasonable port. You see she is equipped to unload herself. That makes her independent.

Next step in the same direction is the crane vessel. She can load and unload her own hull—and you can see what that does to increase traffic on the lakes.

ᵜ ᵜ

And while we're on ships—let's talk about the bulk vessels. Near the beginning of the Century it commonly occurred that a group of men would raise an amount of capital for the purpose of building an ore boat. It was a profitable business, and therefore, many small groups of men banded together to build and operate a vessel—or perhaps two vessels.

This was fine.

But it did have this effect. Oglebay Norton and others, having ore to ship, found themselves dealing with many shipping corporations, each operating a boat or two. You can see the overlapping that did occur—and the gaps—when independent vessels are your carriers. As a solution to this problem—Oglebay Norton—again sticking to its role as coordinator—formed many of these vessels into a coordinated fleet. This occurred in 1920—and with the origins of the business fresh in our minds—and remembering the good Brig *Columbia* which brought down that 132 tons of ore—we called it The Columbia Steamship Company, presently The Columbia Transportation Company.

Today our fleet is made up of bulk vessels, self unloaders, and crane vessels.

[20]

But the race continues as before. Our two new vessels com-missioned last year are of much larger carrying capacity, and they come down at greatly increased speed. And to show you that the race is still on—you should know that a few years ago the best bulk vessel required 7 days for the round trip—today they make the turn-around in about 5.3 days.

❦ ❦

But now, I am a little ahead of my story. Sure we needed big-ger, faster, unloading equipment to unload bigger ships which could now get through the larger channels with more ore. But why did we need ever-increasing ore shipments anyway?—

Well, that's because of Mrs. Higgins—who kept demanding a better pan. She was rid of that big black brute that weighed 14 pounds and cracked if you dropped it. But she wanted to be rid, also, of that chrome trimmed black monster underneath the kettle —that old wood range with the iron eagle feet, holding a small cannon ball. She wanted a substitute for that reeking, dripping wooden ice box. She wanted the pans thinner, too, and lighter and prettier. And she even wanted them smaller on the outside and bigger on the inside.

Next she wanted one of those new fangled horseless carriages, and then tougher armor plate to protect her sons in the First World War.

And from Mrs. Higgins' continuing dissatisfaction came one of the greatest inventions of our times. It began in the month of June, in the Year 1904. In Detroit, a pale, slight young man was trying to coax life into a cantankerous assembly of wheels and gears and shafts that he called simply: a Ford.

In Canajoharie, New York, a man named Arkell was pouring the last of an inherited fortune into one final effort to perfect a method of preserving food in vacuum jars.

At the St. Louis Exposition a brash young scientist named De-Forest had built the tallest structure on the grounds—a steel tower. He said he would use it to send messages without wires.

In Chicago, the son of Abraham Lincoln was building a sleeping car for railroad passengers.

⟦ 21 ⟧

And in Middletown, Ohio, a man with a classical education, with fine clothes and pale hands, was asking Charlie Hook for a job. John Tytus explained that he had majored at Yale in English literature. Charlie explained that they weren't using much English literature just then, in the Armco mills.

It turned out though, that John Tytus got the job he wanted because he had an idea that had always been close to Charlie's heart. Tytus' father owned a paper mill and in it they rolled paper in a continuous strip. The boy couldn't see why steel couldn't be rolled that way, too.

Charlie Hook and everybody in the steel business knew what a lot of grief that idea would lead to.

But from that moment the Armco mills were a laboratory for John Tytus.

With each pass of a slab through the rolls—twenty-two of them to produce a sheet—John Tytus learned something about the art of rolling sheets. Week after week he stood his turn—in twelve hours twelve tons of sheet steel—in his mind he saw a continuous strip of steel in a coil a quarter of a mile long, feeding into a press. Smack! A fender. Smack! A fender. Then Mrs. Higgins could own an automobile.

ಜ ಜ

John Tytus plunged into his experiments like a man possessed. "Machines were built that were as full of bugs as a lumber camp bunk house" but finally they came upon the answer to a continuous hot strip mill.

Sheet now pours out of continuous mills for railroad cars, for automobiles, for canned goods, and—for Mrs. Higgins.

The same kind of pioneering could be told of the development of stainless, seamless tubing, pressure blowing—and the hot top for steel ingots. Concerning this latter there was a time when in pouring a steel ingot you found a great empty crevice in the center of your ingot extending a great distance down from the top—a little like the false bottom in a champagne bottle if you turned it upside down. The hot top is like a cap with an insulating lining containing molten steel. As the ingot cools the

[22]

molten steel in this hot top slowly feeds into the ingot eliminating the crevice and making a sound ingot. The Ferro Engineering Company, an associate of ours, is responsible for this part of steel-making efficiency.

But this is again only one of a hundred and one steel-making milestones along the lakes and the tributaries.

❦ ❦

Now our firm are not makers of steel. But we're proud to draw up a chair at the iron round table as furnishers of raw materials. Because whenever the steel men moved ahead, they called for better ores, purer ores—or more of them. And we have tried to be quick to answer. Consequently, we obtained an agency for the sale of fluorspar, which in addition to use as a flux in steel making, has many chemical and ceramic applications. It means to Mrs. Higgins many things including frosted light bulbs and porcelain for her house to replace the black soapstone kitchen sink and the black iron range.

❦ ❦

We also supply ferro manganese, spiegeleisen and phosphate rock for the steel makers.

❦ ❦

Coal has kept abreast in the same kind of a breakneck race. You can't make iron without coke and you can't make coke without coal. In 1928, Oglebay, Norton began handling the output of other people's coal mines in all important production areas. And, in 1935, we also took over mines ourselves in Ohio and West Virginia.

❦ ❦

Recently Mrs. Higgins began to abandon us along in here in favor of oil and gas. But at the same time—she began plugging in more automatic electric pans and coffee makers and light bulbs —which meant the electric utilities had to turn up the rheostat and pour on more coal, and it had to be purer coal. When they asked for it, we had it for them.

And coal became kind of fancy. The mules went out—and as mining machinery became more efficient we were taking out more

[23]

100 Years of Oglebay Norton

of the impurities and delivering more BTU's from less tonnage. And we dryclean it, launder it, wash it. In 1949, Oglebay, Norton put in the first continuous mining machine in Ohio—and now we're doing everything but wrapping it in cellophane. Fact, the cellophane people—being one of our good customers—are apt to suggest that very thing. But one thing, though, about this business—probably the best thing about it—is the way we all keep running to stay ahead of Mrs. Higgins. The pan we give her next year will be better than this one and it'll cost her still less.

❦ ❦

Mrs. Higgins was worried about us for awhile. She read that we were so busy making her pans we forgot one of the lessons of the early days. She got the idea we had lost sight of our source of raw materials.

❦ ❦

I want to reassure her on that point. We know where our iron ore is coming from for the next hundred years—it will come from Liberia, from Quebec-Labrador, from Venezuela, from Chile, but greatest tonnage will still be shipped down the traditional lakes route from Superior to Erie. For more than twenty years now, far thinking men have known that the rich ores of the upper peninsula and the Mesabi would one day run out. Imbedded in these ranges, however, lies another source of ore that can be said for our times to be inexhaustible. Low grade iron ores called *taconites* and *jaspers*.

It'll take an investment of perhaps a billion privately-owned dollars—some of Mrs. Higgins'—to bring about this new national security, but in a few years millions of tons of iron ore suitable for blast furnaces—made from taconites and jaspers—will be moving down the lakes.

❦ ❦

So you see our generation has faced and met problems just as drastic as our ancestors. And on second thought, if I ever *do* meet Henry Tuttle—or Hewitt or Mather, Rockefeller, Carnegie, or the others, I'll meet them with respect, great respect, but I'll want them to know—we're begging no man's pardon for the state of their lakes in 1954.

And we of Oglebay, Norton are proud to have our seat around the iron round table that has in large measure shaped the course of life in these United States.

❦ ❦

Now here we stand. We're standing on safe ground again—raw materials-wise. However, I'm aware that it's a year of wondering. Never before have we gotten up every morning with such self-probing. Our estimate of the future changes from day to day —as never before. We've all had it good.

Economically we're educated to the teeth these days. So we examine our good fortune suspiciously, carefully, and often—every morning in fact. We study every competent economic survey and report with dark glasses.

What we should really do is go on out Euclid or Clifton or Broadway—way out—and knock on any door—and look at Mrs. Higgins who is sitting on billions of dollars.

❦ ❦

Mrs. Higgins is setting a sixth plate at her dinner table this year —that is, there has been a 60 percent increase in the number of fourth children born to U. S. families since 1940. The population increase expected by 1960 is exciting, because Mrs. Higgins will be shopping for so many new cooking pans. It's true she's waiting right now. She's waiting until the price is right, and she'll decide when that is.

You see, she's just like we are—she has also become economically educated—and her daughter, too. They took the advanced post-graduate seminar—along with you and me—back in 1933. And in fact it would not hurt us to go on the assumption that she got higher grades for the course than we did.

She has the money. But she knows better than any of us when the price is right. And when it is—Mrs. Higgins will buy a better pan—millions of them.

[25]

100 Years of Oglebay Norton

Gentlemen, you've been very good to us Oglebay, Norton people to honor us with your citation and your presence. I am humbly anxious that we have warranted the honor and that we have not tonight violated Henry Tuttle's instructions about conserving your time.

THE END

"Actorum Memores simul affectamus Agenda!"

100 Years of Oglebay Norton

THIS NEWCOMEN ADDRESS, *dealing with the history of Oglebay, Norton and Company on occasion of its 100th Anniversary (1854-1954), was delivered at the "1954 Cleveland Dinner" of The Newcomen Society in North America, held at Cleveland, Ohio, U.S.A., on May 11, 1954.* MR. TAYLOR, *the speaker, was introduced by* CHARLES R. HOOK, *Chairman of the Board, Armco Steel Corporation, Middletown, Ohio; Vice-Chairman of the Cincinnati Committee, in American Newcomen. The dinner was presided over by* GEORGE W. CODRINGTON, *Retired Vice-President and General Manager, Cleveland Diesel Engine Division, General Motors Corporation, Cleveland, Ohio; Chairman of the Cleveland Committee, in this international Society.*

100 Years of Oglebay Norton

AMERICAN NEWCOMEN, *interested always in industrial and economic history, takes satisfaction in this colorful narrative of the life-story, during "100 Years on the Great Lakes," of an enterprise which has contributed in such large measure to the economy of the extended geographical area with which its operations are identified—and has contributed indeed to the American Economy!*

❧ ❧

100 Years of Oglebay Norton

THE NEWCOMEN SOCIETY
in North America

MORE THAN *30 years ago, the late L. F. Loree (1858-1940) of New York, then dean of American railroad presidents, established a group now known as "American Newcomen" and interested in Material History, as distinguished from political history. Its objectives center in the beginnings, growth, development, contributions, and influence of Industry, Transportation, Communication, the Utilities, Mining, Agriculture, Banking, Finance, Economics, Insurance, Education, Invention, and the Law—these and correlated historical fields. In short, the background of those factors which have contributed or are contributing to the progress of Mankind.*

The Newcomen Society in North America is a voluntary association, with headquarters in Uwchlan Township, Chester County, within the fox-hunting countryside of Eastern Pennsylvania and 32 miles West of the City of Philadelphia. Here also is located The Thomas Newcomen Library, a reference collection open for research and dealing with the subjects to which the Society devotes attention.

Meetings are held throughout the United States of America and across Canada at which Newcomen Addresses are presented by leaders in their respective fields. These manuscripts represent a broadest coverage of phases of Material History involved, both American and Canadian.

The approach in most cases has been a life-story of corporate organizations, interpreted through the ambitions, the successes and failures, and the ultimate achievements of those pioneers whose efforts laid the foundations of the particular enterprise.

The Society's name perpetuates the life and work of Thomas Newcomen (1663-1729), the British pioneer, whose valuable contributions in improvements to the newly invented Steam Engine brought him lasting fame in the field of the Mechanic Arts. The Newcomen Engines, whose period of use was from 1712 to 1775, paved a way for the Industrial Revolution. Newcomen's inventive genius preceded by more than 50 years the brilliant work in Steam by the world-famous James Watt.

༝   ༝

Members of American Newcomen, when in Europe, are invited

❦

"The roads you travel so briskly
lead out of dim antiquity,
and you study the past chiefly because
of its bearing on the living present
and its promise for the future."

—LIEUTENANT GENERAL JAMES G. HARBORD,
K.C.M.G., D.S.M., LL.D., U.S. ARMY (RET.)

(1866-1947)

Late American Member of Council at London
The Newcomen Society of England

❦

100 Years of Oglebay Norton

The Wreck of the Oglebay Nortond

POSTSCRIPT

O-N and I

My association with
Oglebay Norton goes back
to my high school days in
Hudson, Ohio. My Father,
M. Dwight Harbaugh, a
Mining Engineer/Geologist, was President of the
American Iron Ore Association, of which Oglebay
Norton was a major member, with offices adjoining
Oglebay Norton's in the Hanna Bldg. in Cleveland,
Ohio.

Commencing at age 16, I sailed on summer vacation
as a Coal Passer, shortly promoted tp Acting
Firemam , on Oglebay Norton's Great Lakes bulk
carrier the SS Joseph H. Frantz. The work was hard
and the food excellent. As Coalpasser I made
$156.00 a month for 8-hous per day 7 days a week.
Promoted to Fireman I got $172.00 per month. This
was a fortune for a high school lad in those days.

I served in the Navy in WW II, attended college on the
GI Bill, and ended up a Civil/Military Engineer.
Throughout my career path I sailed many time on
Oglebay Norton ships.

The Wreck of the Oglebay Nortond

At age 44, in December1971, returning from 5 tours in Vietnam as an Engineer with 'MACV' – Military Assistance Command Vietnam, I saiied as 'Oiler' on the SS Edmund Fitzgerald, 4 years before she sank in November 10, 1975,I knew all the crewmen that went down ith her

I spent my last 4 years before retirement sailng on Oglebay Norton's 1000-ft flagship 'MV Columbia Star', as 'QMED' – Qualified Member Engine Dept. I am now an Oglebay Norton retiree, drawing a pension assumed by their successor Carmeuse Lime Inc.

MV. COLUMBIA STAR

The Wreck of the Oglebay Nortond

SS Edmund Fitzgerald getting up steam for departure from Lorain, Ohio in 1971. Good honest coal smoke with no worries about 'Global Warming'.

The Wreck of the Oglebay Nortond

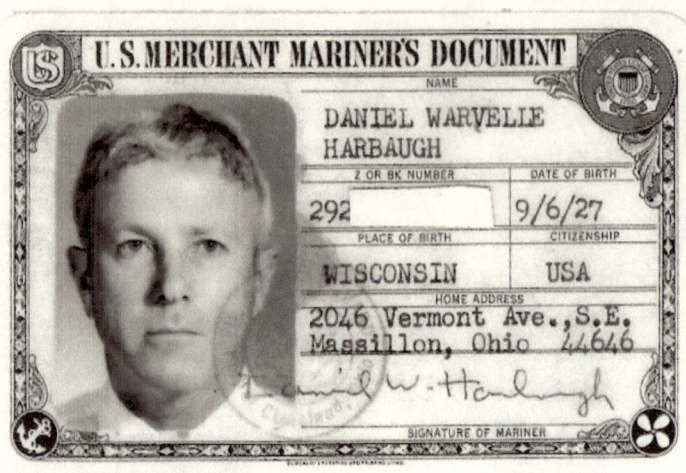

The Wreck of the Oglebay Nortond

The Wreck of the Oglebay Nortond

www.ingramcontent.com/pod-product-compliance
Lightning Source LLC
Chambersburg PA
CBHW022026170526
45157CB00003B/1373

* 9 7 8 1 3 6 5 8 9 9 8 6 7 *